POETRY

&

MYSTICISM

RAÏSSA MARITAIN

INTRODUCTION BY JAMES MATTHEW WILSON

We are grateful to the Philosophical Library for providing us with permission to reprint these essays.

Printed in the United States of America

Set in Baskerville Typesetting

Cover Design: Silk Sheep Studio

Paperback ISBN-13: 978-1-951319-55-7

Non-fiction / Monograph

CONTENTS

James Matthew Wilson

From the perspective of early-twenty-first century America, it may at first prove hard for the reader to grasp the significance of the literary debates that simmered among the intellectuals of Paris nearly a century ago. Curiously, the chief subject of argument was the nature of poetry; the subject only arose in the first place as a consequence of the great revival of Catholic philosophy and letters that was then occurring. And yet, we can trace a direct link between those odd and long forgotten exchanges and the major statements of three popes—John Paul II, Benedict XVI, and Francis—and a multitude of theologians that literature and the other arts of the beautiful are sources of insight and powerful witnesses to the spiritual life. What began as the arcane concern of a few poets, artists, atheist provocateurs and scholarly priests would lead, over the next century, to a renewed conviction, on the part of the Catholic Church, that beauty must save the world.

These two essays by the poet and contemplative, Raïssa Maritain, wife of the great Catholic philosopher Jacques Maritain, may therefore be read with an interest at once historical and evangelical: historical, insofar as they shed light on the particularities and urgent concerns of Catholic thought a century ago; evangelical insofar as they help us better to understand that the fine arts, though possessing a nature and integrity proper to themselves, are bound to open onto the great questions of human life and destined to play a role in the spiritual life of every age. What may seem fairly modest inquiries into the psychology of the poets would eventually bear fruit in our contemporary understanding that what John Paul II called "epiphanies of beauty" matter deeply even to those who may never read a poem.

Four events in French history shaped the concerns and arguments in Maritain's day and will help us understand why she composed these essays. The first had occurred more than two centuries earlier: Jean Racine, the greatest of French poets, its classic playwright of verse tragedy, quit the theater, in 1679, and seems to have returned to a life of strict piety among the Jansenist sect of Port-Royal. Racine's actual reasons for quitting the theater were complicated, but his departure created the appearance of opposition between the theater as a stage of profane immorality and the Church as the altar of sacred devotion. In 1927, the French novelist François Mauriac could still write with empathy regarding the "agonizing fluxes" and the final "renunciation" Racine felt obliged to make. He could do so, because Racine's choice still weighed on the conscience of Catholic writers more than two centuries later. Could a Catholic also be a writer of literature? Or did the faith call for a renunciation of such worldly imaginings?

The question was posed, in Catholic Paris, in the starkest terms. One modern French novelist, Léon Bloy, who was instrumental in the conversion of the Maritains to the Church, took a wicked pleasure in declaring with typical hyperbole, "Art is an aboriginal parasite of the skin of the first serpent . . . One may meet a few rare and ill-fated individuals who are at the same time artists and Christians, but there cannot be a Christian art." Racine's quitting the theater had made art and piety to appear mutually exclusive. Those persons who dared to call themselves Catholics and artists seemed at the least to be flirting with the service of two masters. Indeed, Mauriac's essay that discusses Racine was called *God and Mammon*.

A second, similar historical event also haunted the memory

of French writers at this time. In 1875, Arthur Rimbaud, the visionary, romantic poet who had made of his art a kind of secular religion, abandoned the art altogether. Where Racine had ceased writing poetry in favor of morality and piety, Rimbaud had sought the life of the spirit through poetry and it had ruined him. He abandoned literature for a life of itinerant trade and died at a young age. "It is a mortal error," Jacques Maritain had written in 1926, "to expect from poetry the supersubstantial nourishment of man." If Racine tempted Catholic writers to think of their art as an alliance with the devil, Rimbaud had tempted many to see poetry as an essentially mystical art or as a pathway to the life of religious mystery. His poetry had led, for instance, to the conversion of Paul Claudel, the greatest of French Catholic poets.

Racine and Rimbaud shaped the consciousness of French intellectuals trying to read the signs of their own times, as they struggled to interpret still a third event, what was really a pair of events: the separation of church and state in 1905 and the immense suffering of the French people in the First World War. Catholics were quick to describe the German aggressors in the War as an apos- tate, pagan people; they looked upon the expulsion of the Church from French public life and the triumph of a secular, rationalist, and republican ruling regime as sins that cried out to God for vengeance. French politics had deliberately excluded the spiritual life and the historic influence of the Church; its institutions of education and culture had been given over to scientific positivism. Raïssa would write of her education at the prestigious Sorbonne that the faculty "wished to snuff out all enthusiasm and all faith and all loyalty under the weight of routine and proce- dures." "Truth" was spoken only "between the quotation marks of a disillusioned smile."

After the great destruction and misery of the War, French Catholics, the Maritains among them, sought to redeem France, oldest daughter of the Church that she was, from such guilt. That many French religious, who had been exiled from the country as part of the laws of 1905, returned and then fought and died in the trenches during the War, seemed a sure sign that Catholics were called to restore to the nation to its lost faithfulness. Catholic clergy had died for France. Now, France must remember her historic faith.

This hope for a religious restoration culminated in a fourth and final event, one far smaller in scale than the Great War. The Catholic priest, scholar, and author of many books, Henri Brémond, sparked a vigorous debate in Paris regarding—of all things—poetry. First, he raised the question of "pure poetry": what was poetry in itself with all extrinsic interests cleared away? And, second, he began to speak and write about the relationship between poetry and prayer. Brémond saw poetry as having a self-sufficiency, and autonomy, proper to itself, but he also saw, in his reading of the English romantics, that the greatest poetry seemed to open onto insights akin to those of the religious mystics—of whom, as it happens, he was writing a multivolume history.

Brémond's interventions in Parisian culture might, by themselves, seem arcane, but in the context of the preceding events we see that he and others who engaged his ideas were making a reckoning. Were art and religion in irreducible, demonic tension with one another? Or was poetry indeed a pathway to the spirit, as Rimbaud had once believed? If so, why had the career of Rimbaud miscarried? Could it be that poetry really did have a spiritual vocation, but one that would take the rigor, orthodoxy, and discipline of the Catholic Church to realize? Finally, what could French artists do, while respecting the integrity of their art, to awaken their country from the secular slumber that had proved disastrous for its fortunes?

Asking such questions was made at once more challenging and enticing by another feature of Catholic life at the time. Along with its political defeats in France and elsewhere, the Church had just gone through the "modernist crisis," where currents of secular and liberal Protestant thought threatened to undermine the foundations of Catholic orthodoxy. The Church reacted to the modernist heresies with a tightening of the oversight of its clergy but also with a commitment to educate them according to the rigors of a revived scholastic philosophy and theology, namely that of the great theologian Saint Thomas Aquinas.

Although the Church had endured real crises and serious defeats, it was also undergoing an intellectual revival with Aquinas at its center. Intellectuals in the Church had to toe a careful line, but they also had resources at their disposal that, even a generation earlier, had lain largely neglected. Artists and writers felt a special responsibility in such a context. There was more room for free invention in the arts than in the neo-scholastic theology and philosophy, but that same neo-scholasticism helped such artists to account for themselves, to reckon with the ghosts of Racine and Rimbaud, and to discover a role for the arts of the beautiful in the restoration of the Catholic faith in the modern age.

Maritain's essays collected here show her nimble engagement with all this. Raïssa and Jacques alike believed that the romantic movement in the arts had made poets conscious of their distinctive spiritual purpose. The arts in general, when they were true to their essential nature, served to awaken a people enthralled to the superficial knowledge of the modern sciences to the profound mystery of being. The arts could express the "ontological secret" that irradiated from the interior life of things but which could never be rendered by the surface representations of so-called realism. Photography was mere verisimilitude; modern painting, with its willing disfigurement of surfaces, revealed invisible truths. The nineteenth-century realist novel observed persons and behavior as if they had no interior and no significance; the novels of Mauriac, Bloy and others were pilgrimages of the spirit in the search of the absolute. The neo-classical poetry of the French seventeenth century came to mere wit and courtly amusement, but poetry after Rimbaud pursued what Jacques Maritain called "poetic knowledge" to return the mind to a vision of the real.

In "Sense and Non-Sense in Poetry," Raïssa Maritain considers the way true poetry always transcends its "logical sense" in order to convey a "poetic sense." Poetry is wholly incarnate in the form of the work and yet it also speaks out of the invisible depths of human experience. Poetry is a human thing, but it stirs the human beyond mere "logic" in the direction of the divine. "Poetry is the fruit of a contact of the spirit with reality, which is in itself ineffable, and with the source of reality, which we believe to be God himself in that movement of love which causes him to create images of his beauty." Poetry resembles in this respect mysticism and contemplative prayer—which is the subject of Maritain's first book, *Prayer and Intelligence* (coauthored with Jacques, as was the book in which these essays first appeared).

Even so, poetry is *not* mysticism. It is not a kind of second-rate mysticism, as Brémond at one point suggested, and it is not identical with mysticism (or superior to it), for poetry and mysticism each have their own essence, integrity, and "ontological laws." The prayer of the mystic, after all, ends in silence; the connatural and affective poetic knowledge of the poet ends in the expression of a new word. Nonetheless, she admits, there is an analogy between poet and mystic that helps explain why poetry, far from being a pustule of the devil, really does lead to the cultivation of the spirit, the return to the real, and even to the threshold of the divine mystery of the creator.

Maritain makes clear in these essays that poetry is not "magic." By this, she means to say, it is not a kind of substitute for religion that, unlike divine grace, is subject to the demands of the poet. On the other hand, it does help poet and reader alike enter into a richer vision of reality: to see the world as mystery, created in the image of God's beauty.

When these essays first appeared, they were sometimes misunderstood. T.S. Eliot, a friend and admirer of the Maritains, thought its theorizations could prove positively harmful for practicing poets: "I recommend it warmly to all readers of poetry . . . who are content to read poetry and do not attempt to write it . . . but I advise [poets] against reading the book: it is concerned with matters that they ought to leave alone." He had misunderstood the stakes. Raïssa was not counseling poets how to write but the Church how to become receptive to the knowledge, insight, and evangelical impulse that the arts of their nature provide.

And here lies the evangelical interest of these essays. The writings of both Raïssa and Jacques Maritain helped such theologians as Henri de Lubac and Hans Urs von Balthasar, and later leaders of the Church, to see the centrality of aesthetic experience in the formation of the soul. They also helped them to rediscover that aesthetic experience could be formative of the soul only because beauty, far from being "the ornament of a bourgeois past," was a transcendental property of all being. To know reality we must reckon with the "ontological secret" of form and splendor—in a word, of beauty. This has in turn led to a recovery of the aesthetic dimension of Aquinas's theology—and Aquinas's grasp of the nature of beauty was the most perfect we have known—and of the role of beauty in the Church's tradition writ large.

Poetry is "evangelical" not because it is winsome, appealing, and charming, but because it is a way of encountering reality. Poetry provides true insight on being by way of beauty, precisely because beauty is itself a fundamental dimension of the real. These are truths that the Church's tradition has always borne within itself. One need only to look to the Book of Wisdom or the Gospel of John, or to the theology of Saint Augustine or the Pseudo-Dionysius to see that the Church's understanding of reality is something like a reflection on the splendor of being. And yet, as Racine's troubled relationship with the theater indicates, they are truths that from time to time have become obscured. The seeming fortuity of Racine, Rimbaud, the Great War, and a scholarly priest provoked into speech a great number of writers, Raïssa Maritain among them. She and others helped the Church, Catholic writers, and people everywhere to rediscover the essential role beauty, poetry, and the arts of the beautiful play in the renewal of civilization, in the secret life of the spirit, and in the salvation of mankind.

SENSE AND NON-SENSE IN POETRY

Raïssa Maritain

What I shall attempt to treat of here is *logical sense* and *non-sense in poetry*, and also of *poetic sense*. Logical sense, or rational sense, is not to be required in poetry for its own sake; it seems even to be extrinsic to poetry as such. And yet, in one way or another, to some degree, it always accompanies the poetic work: either in an explicit way, or in appealing implicitly to the cooperation of the intelligence. Otherwise, poetry itself disappears. That is the paradox which we should like to consider.

The *poetic sense* is one with the poetry itself. If I employ this expression here, rather than the word "poetry", it is to indicate that the poetry, or "poetic sense", causes the poem to be, by being the *form* (in Aristotelian language) or the *idea* (in the language of Spinoza) of this body, by giving it a substantial signification, an ontological sense. This *poetic sense* is quite another thing than the intelligible sense, just as the soul of a man is quite another thing than his discourse: and in the poetic work, the poetic sense is inseparable from the formal structure of the work: whether the work be clear or obscure, the poetic sense is there, whatever may become of the intelligible sense; the poetic sense is substantially bound to the form, immanent in the organization of the words, immanent in the poetic form. It cannot be separated from the verbal form which it animates from within. To "tell the story" of a poem, even the clearest of poems, is to abolish the poetry. And the sense one draws from it, in paraphrasing it, is no longer the sense of the poem. The sense of the poem is one with its verbal form.[1] (That certain verbal "correspondences" are possible from one language to another does not contradict this assertion.) This is what first of all distinguishes the poem from all works in the prosaic mode—I do not say from all prose. In the prosaic mode, indeed, the words are almost exclusively only *signs*; they have in themselves only a secondary importance. In poetry, on the other hand, the words are at the same time signs and *objects* (objects that are carriers of images) which are organized in a living and independent body; they cannot give place to synonyms without causing the sense of the poem to suffer or die. That is why the majority of great poets cannot be translated: thus it is with Dante, Racine, Pushkin, Baudelaire, and with many others. The untranslatableness of their work is like that of music, in which the relation of duration and interval cannot change without the work's ceasing to be itself. In the majority of cases, translating a poem causes the poetry to disappear, unless the translation be itself a new poem in sympathy with the first one—one of those "correspondences" in which the intuitions "respond" to each other. Certain poetic elements, however, lend themselves to translation: the play

---

1. Cf. Boris de Schloezer, "La Musique, Art Méconnu," *Mesures*, 15 January, 1937. "This abstraction is only possible in the spoken language because of the fact that the content-form relation is, in this case, a transcendental relation, while in music the content or sense is found to be immanent to the form. But between these two extremes there is poetic language, which can be called 'musical' not insofar as it sounds harmonious and pleases the ear, as is ordinarily supposed, but insofar as what it signifies, its content, is immanent to its form. The pleasure, the sonorous caress, is only an accessory phenomenon, not at all necessary, for a text can be 'musical' in the sense I mean (the only acceptable sense to my way of thinking) and yet be hard on the ear. In this sense, music appears to us as the limit (in the mathematical sense of the term) of poetry; the limit of all the arts, I should even say, for the products of human activity have an aesthetic value precisely insofar as that of which they are signs, their content, is immanent to their form. Now it is only in music that this relation of immanence is found to be realized in all its purity."

of images, the intellectual surprise which their juxtaposition arouses a certain wit, even though the inspiration be tragic, a certain superior and refined "amusement," can pass from one language to another by means of a work of adaptation which does not harm the poetry. Even that kind of poetry which depends on the poignant beauty of a certain quality of intuition and of sentiment, found for example in an Henri Michaux, that poetry also is translatable, though not without some damage . . .

We have said that in poetry the words are at the same time objects and signs, and first of all objects: let us add at once that while being primary objects (object-images), they still remain, and are more than ever signs, and, this time, in their very quality of objects constituting the matter of the poem. Why is this so? Because, of itself, poetry does not consist of a material object turned upon itself, but refers to the universality of beauty and of being, perceived each time, it is true, in an individual existence. But it is by our spiritual and intuitive powers that we refer to being. The words which the poet uses cannot be stripped of their role as signs without depriving the poetry of its essential ties with transcendental beauty. It is not in order to communicate ideas, it is to maintain contact with the universe of intuitiveness that they must thus remain signs. As signs, the words also refer us to all that psychological complexity into which the poet proposes—instinctively—to make us enter, and which he needs to express after his manner, that is to say in a determinate form (and, if the poem is beautiful, in a necessary form). It follows from all this that if one reduces completely the words' function as signs, one enfeebles the poem's power of communication and of domination—at the last extreme one annihilates the poetic sense itself, which is spirit. Thus we can understand why, although logical sense cannot be required in poetry for its own sake, for the sake of clarity of reason,

3

still logical non-sense voluntarily and systematically imposed is incompatible with poetry. So it is that a certain intelligible signification is necessary even for entry into mystery and the unknown. "It is a fact of experience that the feeling for the unknown is not propagated except as beginning from the known," Marcel Raymond has very truly written.[2] And this is without counting the fact that the word, even reduced to its role of image, is already laden with intelligence and spirit: "The image," it has been said, "is only a magical form of the principle of identity."[3] There is a great deal of truth in this formula.

* * *

An unexpected proof of this obscure and secret connection between poetic sense and intelligible sense was given us one day by a curious observation. A poet, a true poet, was giving a lecture on poetry and reading poems of different authors. The lecturer himself was akin to the poets of obscurity, even of non-sense, and especially to Lautréamont. He detested logic in poetry—for quite legitimate reasons; he could not even bear a too highly accentuated aid from rhythm and rhyme, in which he saw a kind of fabrication, as well as an unfair attempt at seduction. Sensitive and rebellious, he was angry at words, forged were words with the hammer of his anger.

And so it happened that he read a poem whose intelligible sense revealed itself quite ingenuously, whose beauty he valued, a poem written by a poet whom he loved—and since he liked neither the intelligibility nor the music of poetry, he massacred the poem, because in reading it he instinctively (and

---

2. *De Baudelaire au Surréalisme.*

3. Pierre Guéguen, *Nouvelles Littéraires*, 1 June, 1929.

also voluntarily) deprived it of all intonation; he read it without accent, in an inhuman manner. And the beautiful poem was stripped of its beauty, it died; the reader had caused it to lose its poetic sense in depriving it of its aura of intelligible signification.

But when he read some other pages, quite close to non-sense, certain texts all charged with a thick and consubstantial obscurity, he lent himself so well to the generating sentiment of these texts that he did not commit a single error in his desire to make the full poetic resonance of them felt. Now here is what seemed to me very remarkable—that in magnifying the poetic sense as he did, he was obliged to read them (and he did it instinctively) in a manner which gave them an appearance of logical sense. By an intonation full of suggestion, by a rhythmic gesticulation, by a certain ordered manner throughout all the long reading, he gave an apparent signification to texts which were quite free of all logical connection, a signification which depended here entirely on the rhythm, the delivery, and on the sensitivity and intelligence of the reader. In short, the reader played here the role of the intelligence in dreams. Although bound by sleep (and that is why the principle of non-contradiction appears to be abolished), the intelligence does not sleep, it penetrates, it surrounds the most incoherent series of images with a mysterious atmosphere of clarity . . .

One can make a complementary experiment by reading a poem lacking all apparent intelligibility without in any way supplementing the non-sense which it claims to be. Read thus, the text will be reduced to a *quantity* of words without qualitative connection among them, that is to say, empty of all poetic sense.

We may add that it will almost always be unjust to read

in this manner even the most obscure of poems, if poem there be. Because the generating sentiment of the poetic work has a very determinate sense for the poet himself (we are not speaking here of automatic writing), to which he related and adjusts his expression, until the poem comes to resemble that sense, which is in itself ineffable. And the poet cannot do that without the aid of the intelligence, however instinctively, in however shadowy a fashion it may act. He will write even his non-senses with a certain secret measure, a certain music; in spite of everything, in spite of himself, he will write with a rhythm of phrase which, if the reader observe it, will give to the poem, at least by intonation, an appearance and even more than an appearance of sense, and intelligible resonance. It is in this sense that we said at the beginning that in one degree or another, in one manner or another, the intelligible sense is always there, making at least an implicit and insidious appeal to the attention of the intelligence.

*   *   *

Why is this so? Because poetry is a human thing. It is born in man in his deepest self, there where all his faculties originate. When it is exteriorized in an object, in a song, in a poem, it must bear the trace of its origin. If the poet, imbued with preconceived and systematic ideas, lay hand upon one or another of its roots to pull it up, upon one or another of its features to efface it, he does an impious thing, he wounds the poem in its process of becoming, and poetry flees through these wounds. To reduce poetry to the simple flow of images is just as arbitrary as to tie it to the reasoning reason. To suppress systematically either the intelligible sense, when it presents itself in the poetic intuition itself, or the expression of the sentiments and of sensibility, is to impair the sincerity and the purity of the inspiration just as surely as if one wished to render the poem didactic by dint of clarity. There exists, without a doubt, the legitimate labor of the poet, which follows the intuition and the conception, but he must know how to construct his work without denaturing anything. No doubt some transposition is necessary, but it is given with the poetic inspiration itself, it is not done afterwards, it is the spontaneous act of the poet. That which goes further is fabrication. And if some great poet should pretend to reduce poetry to that, it is perhaps out of modesty, irony, or sadness.

When that which has moved and concentrated the poet in a profound—and obscure—experience is in itself a supremely intelligible reality, an unbearable light—even though it results in an obscure knowledge of contact and union, which vibrates with the unspeakable complexity of mystery—the poet will tend involuntarily to express himself with a certain clarity, with a high degree of intelligible sense; we have an eminent example of this in the Psalmist.

But if the poet's emotion results from a reality in itself obscure—"obscure as feeling," as Paul Reverdy puts it—he will tend to express himself according to the obscure mode of his initial emotion, like Reverdy himself.

Is that not what Rimbaud said? "The poet is really a stealer of fire . . . *If what he brings back from over there has form, he gives form; if it is unformed, he gives unformedness.*"[4]

---

4. *Lettre du Voyant* (to Paul Demeny, May 15, 1871).

*   *   *

Song and poetry seek to liberate an experience, a substantial knowledge. As knowledge, it seeks an expression; as substantial, it is properly speaking ineffable. That is why it is not expressed in the manner of reasoning, nor of a didactic exposition. Born in a vital experience, life itself, it asks to be expressed by life-bearing signs, signs which will conduct the one who receives them back to the ineffability of the original experience. Since in this contact all the sources of our faculties have been touched, the echo of it ought itself also to be total. We do not at all wish to say here that the poetic work ought to be the mirror of our psychic states. The relation of the poet to his work is not so simple as that. It can say, in the same work,[5] both that "the value of a work exists by reason of the poignant contact of the poet with his destiny," and "that it is no longer a matter of arousing emotion by the more or less pathetic telling of a human-interest story, but as grandly, as purely as it is done in the evening by the sky crackling with stars, by the sea, calm, imposing, tragic, or even a silent drama played by the clouds beneath the sun."

We said a moment ago that to some degree the intelligible sense is always necessary to the poetic sense. Now we are brought back to the other aspect of things, to that obscurity which is also, to some degree, always there. The poetic sense, in short, is not the same as the logical sense, and the poem, born in the obscurity of withdrawal (*recueillement*), is necessarily obscure to some degree, be it only by virtue of "some" instinctive "slip" in the choice of words. Without being incompatible with the intelligible

---

5. *Le Gant de Crin*, Paris, Plon (*Le Roseau d'Or*).

sense, this obscurity subsists in all true poetry, as the soul of the poetry.

But there are all sorts of obscurity. Between the intelligible poetry of a Virgil or a Baudelaire and the non-sense cherished for its own sake in certain surrealist texts, are found all degrees of intelligibility and of obscurity. And the causes of this are diverse. Let us try to analyse some of them.

The principal cause of the obscurity which goes to the point of non-sense is truly, even if the poet is an atheist, of a quality which is impossible not to call religious. A pathetic cause, and one which in our day has erupted with an unprecedented intensity, it is first of all—in Lautréamont, in Rimbaud—the despair of ever-seizing absolute reality, the interior life in its pure liberty; and for others, in the early period of surrealism, it was the hope that suddenly surged up for the rediscovery of that river of the spirit which flows under all our customary activity, of that profound, authentic reality, foreign to all formulae, perceived in those "minutes of abandonment to hidden forces" which vivify. "To attest that the game is not yet up, that all can perhaps be saved—that is the essential of the surrealist message."[6]

In that natural ecstasy in which our soul re-immerses itself, so to speak, in its source, and from which it issues renewed and fortified for the vocation which is its own— whether of poetry or of prayer—the surrealists were caught in the snare of an experience which they could not forget; but, being generally opposed to all religious form and even to the idea of God, they wished to seek therein only the sources of poetry, while they burdened poetry with the duties of sanctity—without the means of sanctity, which

6. Marcel Raymond, *op. cit.*

are essentially the giving of the self. They overwhelmed poetry with this weight, at first. Later, not having obtained from it what they expected, they undervalued it. And then a new despair pushed them toward other spiritual adventures.

From that passive withdrawal into the best part of themselves, which is rare and fecund and which must in some way be deserved, they went on to the passivity of psychological automatism (under the influence of Freud perhaps), of which everyone is capable by the application of the proper techniques. And as for poetry, their error was to believe that its substantial truth is expressed by that psychic automatism, taken as a synonym of the real functioning of thought, and that the image is all-sufficient. But automatism unbinds that which concentration and withdrawal had brought into the unity of life. The liberty so ardently desired presupposes the possession of the self in unity—even though carried away and ravished—not dispersion. "The spirits of the Prophets," says St. Paul, "are subject to the Prophets."[7]

Doubtless automatism voluntarily let loose does not hinder, even facilitates sometimes, the discovery of images, because the imagination is not abolished by automatism

7. St. Paul, *I Cor.* xiv. 32. "And in order," says John of St. Thomas, "that we should not think that man born of the Spirit is pushed by a furious impulse like those whom an evil spirit possesses, the Lord affirms first of all that the Spirit blows where it listeth, in order to signify that to be born of the Spirit brings, rather than takes away, the liberty of election. Indeed, what merit would remain if the Spirit operated in the will not by inspiring it and balancing its inclination, but by violating it? And that is why the Apostle says that 'the spirits of the prophets are subject to the prophets' (when they employ the prophetic spirit in order to announce hidden things), just the contrary of what takes place in delirious ravings." Jean de S. Thomas, *Les Dons du Saint-Esprit*, French translation, 2nd ed., Paris, Téqui, 1950, p. 3.

(not by madness). But these discoveries furnish raw and scattered materials, and the procedure in itself has nothing to do with real liberty of spirit. And, even with the surrealist poets, the automatism is not absolute; the memory, unbound by that passivity, brings back to consciousness what the consciousness had known long before, and forgotten. Thus there is no absolutely pure invention here either. And the spirit of revolt and of indignation, a profound pessimism, resentment against men and things, have animated in a very *significative* manner many texts that are voluntarily obscure.

In a more simply human and more simply poetic order, it could be shown that a certain obscurity follows on an inspiration which proceeds essentially from sentiment or from dreams, and that, on the other hand, the sense of the unsoundable mystery of things, the revelation, the discovery of unwonted analogies, the desire to express, come what may, the ineffable, are the positive and transcendental causes of the obscurity in poetry—sometimes, as in Claudel, by an excess of intellectual concentration.

Another source of obscurity is found in the extreme necessity of renovation forms. This obscurity is especially inevitable in the inventors who arise after a long period of conformism.

When the poet is confronted with the insufficiency of words, when he seeks sonorities yet unknown, when he wishes to give unique expression to a unique perception, he easily admits obscurity and non-sense and composes new words; or he even tries to create a new language. Then the words created answer especially to exigencies of a musical order in the poet's sensibility. But if the case of the poet then appears to resemble the case of the composer, this resemblance remains quite superficial, because with the true composer the work does not escape the control of the spirit, or the necessities of unity and equilibrium, while the poets who create new words by pure instinct obey above all the inclination of their sensibility, if not the spirit of satire or of indignation, and perhaps personal exigencies of transposition.

The case of Joyce is different. His researches have at the same time a plastic and a philological character. He creates new words for thoughts and sensations for which he does not find an expression in the language. Here the non-sense is such for the reader only. In reality, the author writes in a foreign language, known only by himself, but very well known by him.

The non-sense of Mallarmé, on the contrary, is a veritable spoken music (I do not mean to say a song). The pleasure which this music gives is very great. And Mallarmé is very conscious of this "magic." There are musics, and among the most beautiful, which give the impression of being languages. It seems that if one were close enough to the orchestra one could distinguish the words, a whole discourse; but one is never close enough for that, and what reaches us are the vowels without the consonants—it is a magic music which appears to defy us a little. It is the inverse of this which is produced by Mallarmé: one is a little too near to perceive the whole musical development of this orchestrated poetry;[8] one has only the beginnings of it, one hears the separate accents of the instruments— these are words, and they are not words, it is a spoken

8. "The whole language [since the death of Victor Hugo] breaks loose according to a free disjunction into a thousand simple elements; and, as I shall indicate, not without similitude with the multiplicity of cries of an orchestration, which remains verbal." Mallarmé, *Divagation Premiere*.

music—quite the inverse of the musical poetry of Verlaine. Here also the action of the intelligence is present, and intelligence filled, in fact, with occult notions.

*   *   *

And so we are led, in this way, to the poetry in which intelligibility predominates over obscurity.

There is a clarity which comes of ignorance—there is nothing mysterious for the ignorant man who is unaware of his ignorance—from ignorance also of the nature of poetry and of the role of words in poetry. The words are employed in a prosaic manner, that is to say, as simple signs of ideas. And the poet supposes he has acquitted himself in regard to poetry because he has observed some formal rules of versification. Thus it is with didactic poetry, and with a certain neoclassicism.

There is a clarity which comes of naivete, when this is united with great gifts of imagination and simple sentiments. This is especially characteristic of folk poetry.

Another sort of clarity results from the abundance of philosophical and religious ideas united to poetic genius, and from the profundity of their invisceration in the soul. As we noted a moment ago, however, the very richness of this philosophical and religious effort, and the super-abundance of sense itself, can produce obscurity.

Finally, it must be recognized that up to the present, clarity has characterized great mastery, magnificent mastery, that of Homer, of Virgil, of Dante, of Shakespeare, of Racine, of Goethe, of Pushkin, of Baudelaire . . .

The poetic gift is so powerful in them that it consumes and brings to the state of fusion the most resistant materials: the clear and precise knowledges, the most prosaic necessities of the language. Everything burns with these "ravishers of fire," and everything takes the form which the good pleasure of Poetry wishes. Here we find at the same time unheard-of discoveries, and poetry, the light of intuition, and that of intelligence. And this poetry persuades us that the mystery of the sun and of radiant daylight is not less than that of the obscurest night.

* * *

We believe then that a certain intelligibility, like a certain obscurity, subsists in every true poetic work. Intelligibility, obscurity, mark the origin of the work conceived in those depths of the soul where intelligence and desire, intuition and sensibility, imagination and love have their common source . . . Once it begins to emerge from this generative and nourishing center, the work appeals, each time in a different fashion, to those powers of the soul, each of which has its own manner of attaining to the real and expressing it.

The source of poetry and of all creative intuition is in a certain experience which one can call obscure and savory "knowledge," with a thoroughly spiritual savor,[9] for at

9. We read in *Measures* (15 April, 1938) an article by René Daumal, which is of the greatest interest in relation to Hindu poetics. It is moving to find in the Sanskrit texts of the Vedic period this definition of poetry: "*Poetry is a word of which the Savor is the essence.*" If the word proffered by the Poet, has Savor for its essence, it is that the poetic experience, from which this word emanates, is itself a savory knowledge. We say that this savor is entirely spiritual. The Vedic texts say that it is "supernatural, supra-physical" or "unworldly." Thus savor is one of the principal characters of analogy between Poetry and the Mystical Experience. For savor, which seems to be connected with every knowledge by affective connaturality, pertains also to the most elevated of the Gifts of the Holy Spirit, to the Gift of Wisdom, which communicates a savory science,

14

with a properly supernatural savor (Cf. Jean de S. Thomas, *Les Dons du Saint-Esprit*, French trans. by R. Maritain, Paris, Tequi, 1950).

The essence of poetry, M. Daumal continues, possesses certain virtues by which it manifests itself: *Suavity*, that is "a refreshment born of the liquefaction of the spirit;" *Ardor*, that is, "an expansive kindling of the spirit;" *Evidence*: "that which penetrates the spirit with the rapidity of fire in dry wood is Evidence, present with all the savors . . . This third virtue of the savor . . . has as its function *to cause to understand*, while the other two have as a function *to cause to feel*" . . . But Poetry does not cause one to understand in the manner of prose; "prose speaks of something, poetry makes something with words." The poetic sense is not the "literal" sense but the "suggested" sense. "The term *resonance* (Dhvani) is more especially reserved" to this form of signification.

"The suggested sense is different from the literal sense [and as well from the figurative sense]:

"In relation to the auditor, in that the literal sense is perceptible by the simple grammarian, while the suggested sense will not be perceived except by conscious *experience* . . . ; in relation to *the means of apprehension*, in that the literal sense is communicated by the pronouncing of the words (the auditor being passive), whereas the suggested sense will not be seized except by the activity of an exercised intelligence; in relation to the *effect*, in that the literal sense gives only information, whereas the suggested sense provokes Admiration (therefore the enjoyment of the Savor) . . . "

Thus the exigency of the (suggested) sense is rigorous. "Incomplete sense depreciates the Savor." Only intentional non-senses, those deriving from poetic style, are allowable, such as: "The bird Tchakora drinks the rays of the moon . . . "

Answering to all exigencies, "a single word, it is said, when well used and well understood, is the Cow from which may be milked all the desires of this world and of heaven."

The Hindu poetics thus appears to leave less place than ours to a certain obscurity. It would admit Racine much more easily than Mallarmé. This is because for Hindu thought poetry has an essentially ministerial function, having to do with Wisdom and with the supreme contemplative Deliverance. It seems, indeed, that the Vedic books, while making an eminent place for Poetry, consider it above all as a way and a means: "Poetry is a means of aiding our deficient reason to accede to the unveiled teaching of the truth." Thus it is necessary that the Poet should already have taken several steps on the road of this teaching, these depths all is spirit and life, and every poet knows that he penetrates there by a concentration of all his senses into unity, however fleeting it be—and that this is a primary condition of poetic conception. We are taking concentration here in the passive sense of *quietude*, not in the sense of voluntary and active concentration.

This concentration or withdrawal is the first gift which is made to the poet, and it is also a natural disposition which must be cultivated. It is because of this, it is in this sense, I suppose, that Rimbaud wrote: "The first study of the man who wishes to be a poet is knowledge of himself, entire. He seeks his soul, he inspects it, he tries it, learns it."[10]

This withdrawal is a psychological phenomenon *analogically* common to the poetic state and to mystical contemplation. The same is true for the obscure and savory knowledge which accompanies it. It is the resemblance between these states which makes Jean Royère say: "Poetry . . . is religious. Its essential obscurity comes from its being the history of a soul and its wishing to observe the mystery; but this obscurity is luminous . . . "[11] (A curious recollection of the *et nox illuminatio mea in deliciis meis* of Psalm 138.) Robert Desnos does not believe in God, but

---

since his task is to attract us "by offering us a tidbit, a savor to taste."

The value of the poetic experience in itself and of the ends of poetry in its own sphere, leaving aside the legitimate subordinaton of all ends to the final end, does not appear to have been disengaged by Hindu thought and appreciated for itself. That, we believe, is a privilege of the Occident, and of modern times. In a general way one can say that in India the predominant preoccupation with Salvation attracted and absorbed poetry, like philosophy, in theological finalities.

10. *Lettre du Voyant.*

11. *La Phalange*, 1909.

he in turn writes: " . . . no one has a more religious spirit than I . . . "[12] But this is also what made Henri Brémond say, wrongly we believe, that "the poetic activity . . . [is] a confused and maladroit approximation, full of holes and blanks, so much so that the poet indeed is only an evanescent mystic or a mystic *manqué*."[13] There are several confusions in all this, it seems to me. And first of all, it is proper to protest in the name of poetry: poetry is not something *manqué*; to say that it is a mysticism *manqué* is to do it too much and not enough honor. It is not mysticism; it is a particular essence, a being which has its own nature; it has its own origins and its own ontological laws. In the second place, it must be considered that the sort of obscure knowledge or affective experience which is that of poetry does not touch the common source of all that exists in the same manner as does the obscure knowledge of the mystical experience. *All sources are in Thee . . . .* Here, in the mystical experience, the object touched is the uncreated Abysm, God the savior and vivifier, known obscurely as present and united with the soul of him who contemplates; while the obscure knowledge which is that of the Poet, and which touches, as object known, the things and the reality of the word rather than God himself, flows from a union of another order, more or less intense, with God the creator and organizer of nature.

Every great vocation confers, on him who is called, the capacity for a certain union with God, through a particular relation of Him, whose essence transcends the multiplicity of His attributes; and the well-defined vocations are distinguished among themselves by pertaining

---

12. *Revue Européenne*, March, 1924.

13. *Priere et Poésie*, p. 208.

to one or the other of the divine attributes into which the supreme Simplicity is divided in the eyes of the created intelligence.

Poets and other artists, the great inventors and the saints, all draw on the same divine source, but with different dispositions, and according to essentially distinct types of relation to that source. They are all of them imitators of God, but some are specially called to augment the human treasure of beauty and science—they are imitators of God the creator; the others are specially called to enter into the mystery of the Deity itself and to make known in the world, by some image, by some resemblance, the Sanctity of God, in imitation of Jesus Christ, by abnegation of self and of all that is of this world. Nature and grace have qualified workers, who render a mysterious mutual assistance to one another for the raising and spiritualization of humanity. It is quite properly then that the former are called "creators" and the latter "saints."

The results which follow on these diverse callings, these experiences distinct in essence in spirit of their proximity in the same divine source, are, like the callings, quite different, for the poet and for the contemplative. Every time that there is natural or supernatural contemplation, the contemplation is itself its own fruit and its own resting place; and in mystical contemplation properly so called the obscure and savory knowledge attained tends to overflow in immanent acts. In the poetic experience, on the other hand, the obscure experience, if it attains a high degree of intensity, tends to fructify in an object. Thus the poet, returning from his withdrawal into himself, will write a poem; but the mystic, moved, stirred by his God, will intensify his contemplative life (rather it will be intensified in him), and the acts of the virtues and gifts which join him to God: he will love God and men more deeply. The poet finds the plenitude of his joy in *realizing* his inspiration in the creation of a new form. But for him who comes back to the surface of life from the depth of mystical union, it is affliction to become conscious again of images and distinct forms. The feeling of plenitude for the mystics is in the repose of union, of adhesion to God: *Mihi autem adhaerere Deo bonum est.* The poet, on the other hand, would find perfect joy in the adequacy of the created form to the creative inspiration.

*　　*　　*

But if the mystic is at the same time a poet, what will be in him the existential relations of the poetic gifts and the mystical gifts? It would be a good and useful thing to be able to penetrate this mystery of life. It is in any case certain that these diverse gifts furnish a favorable climate to one another. At the moment when that binding of the powers of the soul which is characteristic of the mystical experience is relaxed, and the mystical concentration or withdrawal is about to terminate, it often happens that it gives way to poetic activity; and that ought not to surprise us, since the whole soul is enlivened by union with God. This is seen clearly in the case of the holy prophets, Moses, Isaiah, David, and the others; and in the case of the great contemplatives like Seuss, Ruysbroeck, Theresa of Avila, John of the Cross, to cite only well-known names. Contemplation does not necessarily produce poets, but these great mystics were also poets, whom the experience of divine things had exalted. According to the multitude of their gifts they have had the power of communicating to us a little of their ineffable experience.

But it also happens that the poet passes from poetic withdrawal to mystical withdrawal. This passage is doubtless accomplished by the agency of a certain enthusiasm and a certain passivity of spirit which renders the poet more apt to receive the divine impressions. The Bible offers us an example of this kind in the Second Book of Kings, and St. Thomas refers to it in the *Summa Theologica*:[14] "Jehosaphat having inquired of Elisha concerning the future, and the spirit of prophecy having failed him, Elisha had a harp-player brought in. *And while this man sang to the harp the hand of Jehovah was upon Elisha and he said: Thus saith the Lord* . . . "[15] It seems then that the spirit of the Prophet was favorably disposed by the music and poetry to receive the light of God, present but invisible to the distraught and divided soul. And what is true of prophecy can also be true of contemplation.

The fact is that when the poet passes from the state of poetic withdrawal, the source of images and forms, to the mystical sleep, images and forms are lost, drunk up by the silence of the soul as rain is drunk up by the sea. The poet has perhaps lost his poem, but in the scale of absolute values that is an inestimable gain.

It is, then, the habit of a certain withdrawal, of a certain sleep of the faculties, of a certain interior silence, which disposes the poet sometimes to divine influences, sometimes to the keen perception of natural causes: "When the soul is abstracted from the sense," says St. Thomas, "it becomes more apt to receive the influence of spiritual substances and also to follow the subtle movements which are born in the imagination from the impression of natural causes,

---

14. *Sum. Theol.*, II-II, 171, a, 2, s. c.

15. II Kings, III, 15.

something which is very difficult when it is absorbed by sensible things."[16]

One sees in this way how serious it would be for a poet not to have from poetry a respect which is sacred, for him to let his gifts be contaminated by any impurity; not only would art thus be turned aside from its proper ends, but also the poet would be prevented from acceding to the contemplative state—which ought to be much more frequently enjoyed by him than it is, and toward which, as we have just seen, he is naturally disposed.[17] For every elevated nature there is moreover a law of transcendence which alone assures the stability of perfection. Goethe has given an admirable formulation of it: "Everything that is perfect in its species," he says, "must rise above its species, become something else, an incomparable being."

These vital relations between the mystical order and the poetic order still leave intact, however, the real distinctness of their essence. On a general level, in the order of mystical contemplation, it is a matter above all of knowing and loving—of knowing *in order to* love. No doubt in the case of poetry a certain knowledge of the created world and of the enigmatic relations among beings is involved, but all this knowledge, which is a knowledge by connaturality, does not tend of itself towards love; it tends toward

---

16. *Sum. Theol.*, 11-11, 172, I, ad. I. "Poetry," writes Jean Cocteau, "predisposes, then, to the supernatural. The hyper-sensible atmosphere in which it envelopes us sharpens our secret senses, and our antennae plunge into depths of which our official senses are ignorant." *Le Rappel a Ordre*, Paris, Stock, 1926, p. 219.

17. "The only true source of art is in our hearts, the language of a pure and candid soul . . . " says C. D. Friedrich, the painter and poet of the finest epoch of German romanticism. "Every authentic work is conceived in a sacred hour, born in a blessed hour; an interior impulsion creates it, often without the artist's knowing."

the creation of beautiful works, in the case of the poet toward the making of a work in words; and these words are interrelated in such a way that they act, as the flute moved to sound by the breath, like an instrument of the poetic state. Thus the poem is a vehicle of poetic inspiration as the flute is a vehicle of music, the painter's brush a vehicle of vision.[18]

Poetry is the fruit of a contact of the spirit with reality, which is in itself ineffable, and with the source of reality, which we believe to be God Himself in that movement of love which causes Him to create images of his beauty. That which is thus conceived in the mysterious retreats of being is expressed with a certain savory illogic, which is not non-sense but a superabundance of sense.

Song, poetry in all its forms, seeks, as we said above, to liberate a substantial experience. (And perhaps also, because of that, the life of a saint is Poetry . . .)

The brooding repose which is provided by such an experience acts as a refreshing bath, a rejuvenation and purification of the spirit. Is that the secret principle of Aristotelian catharsis? We cannot esteem too highly the profundity of the quiet which all our faculties then enjoy. It is a concentration of all the energies of the soul, but a peaceful, tranquil concentration, which involves no tension; the soul enters into its repose, in this place of refreshment and of peace superior to any feeling.[19] It dies "the death of the

---

18. "Poetry is the attempt to represent, or to reconstitute by means of articulated language, those things or that thing which cries, tears, caresses, kisses, sighs, etc., try obscurely to express, and which certain objects in which there is an appearance of life or of supposed design seem to wish to express." Paul Valéry.

19. We read in *Measures* (15 July 1917) a study of Heidegger on Holderlin in which we find a remarkable confirmation of the reflections offered

Angels," but only to revive in exaltation and enthusiasm, in that state which is wrongly called "inspiration," because inspiration was nothing other, indeed, than this very repose itself, in which it escaped from sight. Now the mind, reinvigorated and enlivened, enters into a happy activity, so easy that everything seems to be given to it at once and, as it were, from outside. In reality, everything was there, in the shadow, hidden in the spirit and in the blood; everything that is going to be manifested in operation was there, but we knew it not. We knew neither how to discover it nor how to make use of it before having reimmersed ourselves in those tranquil depths.

Such is, we believe, the course of poetic sense, in itself free and self-sufficient, and of what it inevitably brings with it in the way of logical *sense* and, at the same time, *non-sense*.

---

here: "In poetry," says Heidegger, explaining the thought of Holderlin, "man is concentrated upon the depth of his human reality. In it he accedes to quietude; not at all, it is true, to the illusory quietude of in-activity and emptiness of thought, but to that infinite quietude in which all the energies are mutually in action."

Magic, Poetry, and Mysticism

Raïssa Maritain

We regret not to have been acquainted, before writing our study "Sense and Non-sense in Poetry," with the important works which Albert Béguin has devoted to the romantic poets. The two volumes which treat of "The Romantic Soul and the Dream," and the essay on "Gérard de Nerval" followed by "Poetry and Mysticism" illustrate and corroborate in so significant a manner several of the views presented in this little book that we should like in connection with them to take up again and complete several of the points treated in our study.

In "Poetry and Mysticism," Albert Béguin writes that "the aesthetics which has been elaborated through symbolism and surrealism . . . clearly attributes to art an efficacy which is quite close to that which one recognizes in magical powers, in mystical efforts, and in the contemplations of the speculative intellect."

We think, and we have tried to show, that poetry is distinct in nature from mysticism, and that the kind of knowledge which belongs to it, affective knowledge, turned toward the creation of a new object, is also distinct from speculative knowledge, which is objective union with the reality known. I shall return later to the question of the relations between poetry and mysticism; I should like first to say a few words about the relation between "magical powers" and poetry.

The search for magical powers has been a perpetual temptation for poets: a fallacious seduction which has caused those whom it has led into its blind alley to lose first of all the disinterestedness essential to any activity of the spirit, and then the very taste for poetic creation. Of this temptation Gérard de Nerval was so conscious that he was determined to triumph over it "by an admirable effort of will;"[1] a temptation which Rimbaud finally escaped, but at what a price—by renouncing poetry itself: no doubt "because it was evil" . . . "this ambition to conquer exceptional powers," but also, one may believe, because of the discouraging clarity with which he rapidly saw that poetry does not confer such powers. Nevertheless, indefatigable, in spite of all the disappointments, poets return to their search. What is it that they seek, precisely? What are the "powers" so ardently coveted? They would like to force the gates of the mystery which penetrates us and envelopes us on all sides and to create beings, or act upon created beings, by efficacious signs, as if by sorcery. And to do that, in some cases, by a science of the arrangements of letters and words in accordance with the teaching of the Cabala. For Mallarmé, the most efficacious of these arrangements is the poem.

But the gates of mystery cannot be forced; it is necessary to give oneself in order to enter into the house of God or that of the devil. There is no other recipe; and even so, one is not always sure of being received.

As for the fabrication of a poem in the capacity of a charm, according to some occult science, that is a questionable kind of sorcery; in any case it has but little to do with the ways of knowledge, of wisdom and of beauty. May we not acknowledge how much of poetry a great poet like Mallarmé lost in his desperate calculations, and that for

---

1. A. Béguin, *Gérard de Nerval*, Paris, Stock, 1936

no efficacious magic, for no secret science to be left to the poets his successors. Such a misfortune did not occur to Baudelaire, nor to Edgar Allan Poe, because they wished to know no other alchemy than that which is in the service of poetry itself.

Poe, however, believed in the "power of the word." He even gave this title to one of his stories, and M. Roland de Renéville sees in that a very important testimony in favor of the magical powers of poetry: "Edgar Poe," he writes, "did not fail to reveal the knowledge he had of the occult possibilities of language. In the story entitled 'The Power of Words,' he refers to 'a true philosophy' to affirm that all movement is creative, that the source of all movement is thought, that, finally, the source of all thought is God." [2] Does the poet not make the two "spirits" of his dialogue discuss the material power of the word?

> OINOS: But why, Agathos, do you weep—and why, oh why do your wings droop as we hover above this fair star—which is the greenest and yet most terrible of all we have encountered in our flight? Its brilliant flowers look like a fair dream—but its fierce volcanoes like the passions of a turbulent heart.

> AGATHOS: They *are*!—they *are*! This wild star—it is no three centuries since, with clasped hands, and with streaming eyes, at the feet of my beloved—I spoke it— with a few passionate sentences—into birth. Its brilliant flowers *are* the dearest of all unfulfilled dreams, and its raging volcanoes *are* the passions of the most turbulent and unhallowed of hearts.

---

2. Roland de Renéville, *L'Expérience Poétique*, Paris, Gallimard, 1938.

Well then, does this text really refer to a magical conception of poetry and of the word? I do not believe so. What we have to do with here, as in *Eureka*, is a pantheistic philosophy and cosmology, in which all movement and every action participate in the efficacy of a divine action, the effects of which, however, are no more knowable to us than the divine essence itself. Actually, it is after death that the disincarnated personages of Poe's dialogue discover the creative effects—which answer to no design premeditated by them—of words expressing their terrestrial "dreams" and "passions." I hardly see a place in Poe's cosmology for researches leading to magical formulae. And still less in his poetry, which was always perfectly free of any anxiety of this order, and of which he would never have wished to make an instrument of "power." Poe was a perfectly disinterested spirit, he was glad of a discovery which gave him, he believed, a true knowledge of the universe; and it is in its beauty, not in some efficacy or other, that he saw the proof of its verity. "To the few who love me and whom I love," he says in the dedication of *Eureka*, "to those who feel rather than to those who think—to the dreamers and those who put faith in dreams as in the only realities—I offer this Book of Truths, not in its character of Truth-Teller, but for the Beauty that abounds in its Truth [Baudelaire and Poe still dare to use these capital letters]; constituting it true."

To affirm the efficacy, infinitely reverberated—up to "the throne of the Divinity," as Poe says—of the least spiritual movement and of the least spiritual act, in no wise engages one in the ways of magic. It is an attitude which justifies itself in the eyes of the scientist, as of the poet and the mystic. Following Poe and Baudelaire, we can cite Léon Bloy, who loved them so much: "A given movement of Grace, which saves me from a grave peril, could have been determined by a given act of love accomplished this morning or five hundred years ago by a very obscure man whose soul corresponded mysteriously to mine, and who thus received his reward . . . What one calls free will is like those common flowers whose winged seeds are carried by the wind, enormous distances sometimes, and in all directions, to plant one knows not what mountains or what valleys. The revelation of these prodigies will be the spectacle of a minute which will last for eternity."[3] And again, in *Le Désespéré*: "Every man who produces a free act protects his personality to the infinite. If he gives a coin to a poor man ungraciously, that coin pierces the hand of the poor man, falls, pierces the earth, bores holes in the suns, traverses the firmament, and compromises the universe. If he commits an impure act, perhaps he darkens thousands of hearts that he does not know, that correspond mysteriously to him and that have need that that man be pure, as a traveller dying of thirst needs the glass of the water mentioned in the Gospel. A charitable act, a movement of true pity, sings divine praises in his name, from Adam to the end of the ages, it cures the sick, consoles the desperate, appeases the tempests, ransoms the captives, converts the infidels, and protects the human race."

In its pure line poetry has no magic power other than that of "charming" and seducing, of "enchanting" and moving, of taming hearts, of communicating to them the appeals and presences, and all that experience of the world and all that hidden reality which the poet himself has experienced.[4] Beyond that, in the line of "powers," it is

---

3. *Méditations d'un Solitaire*, Paris, Mercure de France.

4. Cf. Jacques Maritain, "Signe et Symbole," *Revue Thomiste*, April, 1938. (*Quatre Essais sur l'Esprit*, 1939)—"It is, it seems, by virtue of such

no longer poetry but conniving with forces that are suspect and in the end disappointing as a lie. But in the immaculate line of its own experience Poetry has exceedingly more important powers. Through it the poet learns that way which "goes toward the interior" of which Novalis speaks, and he thus approaches, more or less, ultimate Reality.

For the poet as for the mystic, all avaricious research is a grave fault which scares away the Gifts. But he who has received them and keeps them in a disinterested heart receives in his turn the grace of giving, and he abounds in generous works, the only power the ambition for which causes neither the poet nor the saint to fall. The German and French romantics and the surrealists tried more or less innocently to seek for magical powers. It was sometimes "the hope of an absolute knowledge which for them would be more and better than a simple 'knowledge': an 'unlimited power,' the magical instrument of a redemption of nature."[5] And sometimes it was the desire to remake the world, which disappointed them, according to their own wish. But "since we could not, in order to equal God, become creators," writes Moritz in his *Journal of a Visionary*,[6] "we made ourselves destroyers, we created backwards, since we could not create in the direction of the future. We made for ourselves a universe of destruction, and then, with a tender complacency, we contemplated our work in history, in tragedy, and in our poems." A singular prescience . . . At the origin of such

a slipping that the primitives and the partisans of poetry-magic confound the *presence of cognoscibility* of the signified in the sign with a *physical presence* and an operative efficacy."

5. A. Béguin, *L'Ame Romantique et le Rêve*, Marseille, éditions des Cahiers du Sud, 1937.

6. Quoted by A. Béguin, *ibid.*

a deviation, however, there is the dazzlement of a real experience, in the heart of man, of that which surpasses man. We have said that poetic knowledge does not in itself tend toward love, any more, for that matter, than scientific knowledge; but it must be added that all knowledge which is not finally turned toward loving is by that very fact a source of death. Thus the poet in whom there does not arise the enthusiasm and the passionate desire "to rejoin the essential unity . . . as well in the contemplation of the exterior spectacle as in the apprehension of the obscure data of the interior world," gives way almost necessarily, says G. H. von Schubert, "to another movement similar to that which drags man into the abyss. Like Phaeton, the capricious egoism of man wants to possess itself of the chariot of God: he has wished to create for himself that interior enthusiasm which God alone can create."

Poetry and Mysticism

To divert the poetic experience or the mystical experience towards oneself is to offend the heart of God and of things and cause all real substance to vanish in illusion. But when the poet renounces the vain search after magical powers and is willing to submit "to that orientation of his entire being towards a reality which surpasses exterior reality" from which precisely, according to Albert Béguin, recent poetry has received its distinctive character, he enters into true mysteries, and advances in the fruitful and non-deceptive line of his own discoveries. I shall quote a fine page from Albert Béguin which seems to me to describe felicitously the poetic enterprise:

> If the poet abandons himself to this double flow of images, those which come to him from the surrounding spectacle deprive the sensible world of its reality, through a kind of dizziness, render it transparent, assimilate it to a system of symbols which means more than themselves . . .[7]

Indeed it is difficult with the experience so described to know whether it is the most mystical of poetic graces, or the most poetic of mystical graces. Not that we have here a first undifferentiated moment from which the two ways, the poetic and the mystic, would open out; but there are, at this level, two experiences so close to each other (I do not mean that they are always given together, quite the contrary) that there is hardly an idiom which will suffice to differentiate them. But what follows quite naturally from the one or the other reveals the nature of the starting point.

However that may be, the whole of the text which we are citing clearly concerns the poetic experience. And one could hardly insist too much on the importance, in a way infinite, of the intuition which thus reveals to the poet the significative value of things, become communicative of more than they themselves are:

> "And the other [images], those which arise from the depths of the being and finally come to correspond with these symbols, compose with them a song which speaks of a realm beyond the real, evoke the paradise of the

---

7. "The originals of the images and forms which the language of dreams, poetry, and prophecy employs are found in the Nature which surrounds us and which appears to us like a world of Dream incarnate: like a prophetic language whose hieroglyphs were beings and forms." G. H. von Schubert, quoted in *L'Ame Romantique*, I, 206.

primitive union, and remind the soul of its mysterious relations." This song which without yet being formulated is composed in the depths of the soul, and which demands to come out later, to be sung—here we recognize the poetic experience properly so called oriented from the beginning towards expression. "At the height of the poetic experience the frontiers between an exterior and an interior world disappear; all is image, offered to the free disposition of a spirit which recomposes according to its own wish the order of everything given. The poet re-makes from what is given him a universe suiting his own exigencies, according to his pleasure, conforming himself only to the laws of that euphoria which is aroused in him by this rhythm, that sonorous echo, that association of forms and colors." Here the poet is in his own realm, here all is submitted to his laws, here he can never be too ambitious; here he can be 'a true god,' if he is Baudelaire . . . [8]

"But, at this sovereign point, the spirit ceases to consider itself as the author of the song in which it finds its felicity; it seems to perceive a voice which is no longer its own. That which speaks is not itself but another *who stirs in the depths*, in a symphony which responds to the stroke of its bow." It is thus that every true poet goes—by his own experience of those depths where, as we noted above, all is spirit and life—from the visible to the invisible, and from images of the real to the reality without images, from which he returns, however, with words, sounds, forms, and colors.

Thus the question naturally arises concerning the

---

8. Rimbaud, *Lettre du Voyant.*

relations between Poetry and Mysticism. As to their resemblance and their essential distinction, I have already explained what seems to me to be true; I should like to bring up again here the points of convergence which particularly strike me between M. Albert Béguin's conclusions and my own.

"Call to unity—descent into the regions where the self is renounced in favor of a presence which it perceives within itself—efficacious action of the image: one cannot help, in the first place, noticing singular resemblances between these definitions and those which it is possible to give of the mystical experience."

It is true, the mystic also thirsts for unity and union: unity of all his faculties in peace, union of all his being with God. He too, he especially, frequents "the road which goes toward the interior," up to those mysterious sources where he finds a God more intimate to him that himself. He also feels the need of images, in the meditation which precedes contemplation. And when he finds himself again among us, it is rare that he does not, under the pressure of the abundance of his riches, experience the need of using song and the spoken word to try to communicate the ineffable, to announce to all the presence of God and his goodness—*in aeternum cantabo!* But is the resemblance so perfect that "every boundary between mysticism and poetry must be effaced, and the latter be made the privileged vessel of spiritual ambitions? It is strange, if poetry and mysticism are indistinguishable . . . that all the poets should have the feeling of that *great defeat which perpetuates itself* and of which Aragon once spoke."

Such a feeling, quite different from a simple experience of the internal limitations of art, is it true that *all poets* necessarily experience it? It doubtless occurs that more frequently as the consciousness which poetry acquires of itself turns increasingly to the pure, unlimited desire for poetic knowledge, with which other hopes of the spirit come almost inevitably to be mixed. This feeling of disappointment, in any case, appears to be a distinctive characteristic of essential importance, and sufficient to show, even if it were the only thing, that poetry is not mysticism, and that the poet is preparing bitter disappointments for himself if he demands of Poetry that plenitude of spiritual knowledge which is found at the end of the ascetic and mystic wars. The mystics have never spoken of "that great defeat." It is because they have experimental knowledge, more or less frequent, more or less profound, of that union with God which approaches the perfect Unity. There is the source of their joy; outside of that nothing matters to them (at least for themselves), "outside of that is extreme misery," as one of them, Gerlac Peters, has put it. Whatever otherwise are the trials of barrenness and denudation, the frightful nights that the soul traverses in the quest for union, even at the height of suffering it is never disappointed, provided that it has to do with God and not with men. The plenitude of peace in the mystic, whether it be triumphant or subjacent to terrible combats, proves that he is not mistaken in proposing to attain Unity by the ways of sanctity. If Poetry fulfilled our desires to this degree there would be no "defeat that perpetuates itself;" nor would there be if one did not demand of poetry that it go up to the end of a way where, in any case, it cannot arrive alone. The error, here, witnesses moreover to the grandeur of Poetry, it is the proof of the kinship in the same divine source of the experience of the poet and that of the mystic. But all that poets and mystics have taught us about these things permits us to say, we believe, as we have done above,[9] that if they draw from the same source, it is, however, with different dispositions, and according to essentially distinct types of relation to that Source.

In the exemplary case of a Rimbaud or a Gérard de Nerval, there is more of philosophical error than of pride. But it is an error so dearly paid for that they believed themselves chastised for their audacity and finally retired into silence or remorse. In such a case "the final silence of the poet is a silence of the vanquished one who is resigned; that of the mystics is the peace of him who has achieved the goal of his adventure."[10] No, the resemblance between mysticism and poetry is not an identity; it does not efface their frontiers, though those frontiers are incessantly traversed (especially in the order of natural mysticism) by currents in one direction and the other.

After having insisted on the resemblances, M. Roland de Renéville, in the important book which he has recently published on *The Poetic Experience*, adds with force: "All the same, so many accords, so many coincidences, must give way before the unique [unique it is not, according to our opinion] but fundamental difference which separates the poetic experience from the mystical experience: *while the poet progresses toward the Word, the mystic tends toward Silence.* The poet identifies himself with the forces of the manifest universe, while the mystic traverses them and tries to unite with the immutable and unlimited power of the absolute behind them."

Although it very often happens that the mystic feels the need of describing his experience, the fact remains that for him the expression is not a means of completing the

---

9. *Sense and Non-Sense in Poetry*, pp. 19-21.

10. A. Béguin, "Poésie et Mystique," annex to *Gérard de Nerval.*

experience, is in no way necessary to its conclusion and perfection; it is only a result of superabundance, a generous attempt at communication.

For the poet, on the contrary, the expression is a vital part of his experience, and as it were the fruit of that experience. As Jacques Maritain shows below, "poetic knowledge, which is at the minimum of knowledge but at the maximum of germinative virtuality . . . will only be completely objectified in the work;" and although there can be a poetic experience without a poem, "there is no poetic experience without the secret germ of a poem, however tiny it be." "The necessity of form," says Albert Béguin, "cannot be an accessory or secondary thing in poetry; and that is to say that the realm of poetry, of art, never coincides perfectly with that of mysticism . . . Whatever value one attributes to the poetic act, it remains an act submitted to the necessity of form . . . It ends at the word, and even though convinced that the word has no meaning except by allusion to the Night he has glimpsed, the poet cannot, without ceasing to be a poet, go beyond the word. The mystic tends towards silence, and all that is truly important in his eyes surpasses the articulated word," and even, we shall say, every affirmative mode of expression—that is why negative theology is the ultimate theology in which he finds his reposes, before the Silence which is, itself, the best praise of God in the shadows of the Faith: *Silentium tibi laus.*

It must be recognized that "the most miraculous poetry approaches only remotely the regions of mystical certitude: it is also a matter of its having a different function," and therefore a different nature, a different end. "The roads are diverse by which we seek to become aware of our purest being. To those who are destined to hear its message, poetry appears clothed with a supreme dignity . . . It is the only means that we can glimpse [let us say that it is one of the two great means, the second being precisely the mystical way of union with God, with all that is involved in this way in the moral and religious order] of giving harmony to our entire being, and of creating with the same stroke harmony between our being and all that is not our being. That is what we call beauty and form, which is neither more exterior nor less really a warning and a manifestation than what we call our interior life."[11]

Let us say in conclusion that when it is a matter of mysticism and poetry, however firmly persuaded one may be of the diversity of their essences, one cannot read without emotion the beautiful texts in which all these riches are confounded and which the poets give us, they who are not charged with distinguishing . . . I think for example of that page of Lautréamont: "Poetry announces the relations that exist between the first principles and the secondary truths of life . . . Poetry discovers the laws in virtue of which theoretical politics, universal peace, are living things . . . We are far from fabricators of odes, merchants of epigrams against the divinity. Let us return to Confucius, to Buddha, to Socrates, to Jesus Christ . . . who travelled the villages suffering from hunger."[12]

Everything obliges us to maintain the differences—and first of all between moralists and God; then between poetry and mysticism. But if the Poet confounds everything, would it not be because in him the formative powers of the world and of the word act together with the divine

---

11. A. Béguin, *ibid.*

12. "Preface," *Poésies*, May, 1870 (sometimes referred to as *Préface a e un livre futur*).

attraction towards pacification and illumination of the spirit, toward mystical knowledge and union? We must believe, since the poets tell us that they have discovered in their nocturnal navigations or divagations a Kingdom greater than the world, that an angel is pleased sometimes to tip their bark. So that they take a little "of that water" of which the Gospel speaks and do not get away without some inquietude, and some great and mysterious desire.

Printed in the USA
CPSIA information can be obtained
at www.ICGtesting.com
JSHW011126061223
52979JS00014B/314

9 781951 319557